Calling Out – The Course Participant's Guide

Seven Sessions to Gain Confidence in Sharing Your Faith

J. JOH

Authentic

Cover design by David Lund.
Print Management by Adare Carwin

Contents

Introduction   4

Study 1 – Foundations for Mission – The Big Picture   5

Study 2 – The Building Blocks of Mission: Part 1   10

Study 3 – The Building Blocks of Mission: Part 2   16

Study 4 – Why We Should Call Out . . . And Why We Don't   21

Study 5 – The 'Where' of Mission – Sharing Our Faith Here,
There and Everywhere   27

Study 6 – The Seven Pillars of Mission: Part 1   35

Study 7 – The Seven Pillars of Mission: Part 2   41

Final Word   47

Introduction

My great longing is to see people come to know Jesus Christ. You can call it 'being born again', 'converted', 'making a commitment'; the words don't matter as long as there is the reality of a life-changing switch from being separated from God to knowing him personally through Jesus Christ. For over twenty-five years my life has focused on communicating the great message that in Jesus Christ there is a way for men, women and children to come to know God as Friend and Saviour. I believe that this yearning of mine to reach out to people reflects, in some way, the great desire of God himself. The Bible teaches that God calls out to all people to turn to him. In sharing the good news about Jesus Christ all we are doing is calling out with God.

Foundations for Mission –
The Big Picture

Introduction

Imagine you are working for a big corporation. One day you are summoned to your boss's office, given a pile of envelopes and instructed to go out into the streets and hand them out to people. Now you might obey. However, your enthusiasm might be greater if you knew what was in the envelopes and why you were handing them out.

Our churches try to encourage us to go and talk to people about Christ or invite them to meetings. The fact is, though, that things are easier all round if we know why we are doing it – understanding the 'big picture' helps.

The Big Picture explains why we should tell people about Jesus. Indeed it goes a long way to explaining who Jesus is. Actually, unless we are aware of how we and Jesus fit into the scheme of things our witness may sound rather flat and two dimensional.

The good news of Jesus is not just a series of facts, it is part of the long history of God's dealings with the human race. The Big Picture is so important that in my book *Calling Out* I devoted the first seven chapters to it. Here, in this study, I want to sketch out a rough outline of it.

EXPLORATION

In *Calling Out* I pointed out that in the Bible's Big Picture there were seven major episodes in the history of God's dealings with human beings. I defined these as follows:
  1. God's Good Earth
  2. The Great Rebellion and its Consequences
  3. The Rescue Begins
  4. Jesus: the Great Intervention
  5. The Resurrection: History's Turning Point
  6. The Unfinished Story
  7. The Final Victory

Trying to write a single study to cover all of these was not easy! There were two possibilities. One was to try to skim through the Bible from Genesis to Revelation looking at some of the major themes, but even reducing the Big Picture as much as possible still made for a lot of page turning – something that was hardly appropriate for an introductory study. The alternative, which I have adopted here, is to take a passage in the New Testament that looks at the whole history of God's dealing with the human race and use that as the basis of the study.

Paul's letter to the Ephesians is famous for offering an awesome panorama, almost an aerial view, of history. In Ephesians 1 and 2 you can find references to all the episodes of God's dealings with the human race.

Read, at a single go, **Ephesians 1:3–2:13**.

Episode 1: God's Good Earth

At the very start of the Bible we read in Genesis how God created the universe. A critical point is that, as it was created, everything is repeatedly declared to be good and excellent. In the beginning the relationships between humankind and God, between humankind and the natural world, and within humankind are shown as being perfect and harmonious.

Read **Ephesians 1:4–5 and 1:9–11**

- There are two styles of management; one is where events control us ('crisis management') and the other is where we control events. From these verses how does God control the universe?
- What do we learn from these verses about God's power?
- This passage talks about how God makes plans and purposes. Does Paul see this as being something to puzzle over or something to rejoice at? Is there a lesson here for us?
- What do we learn here about God's feelings towards the human race?

Episode 2: The Great Rebellion and Its Consequences

In Genesis 3 we learn how, when faced with temptation, Adam and Eve rebelled against God. The consequence of this was that sin came into our world and we became separated from God. Ever since then humanity has been in rebellion against God – with disastrous consequences.

Read **Ephesians 2:1–3**.

- What is Paul's verdict on the state of the human race?
- Who has been affected by sin? To what extent?

* What does this passage say to those who believe that all that human beings need to sort themselves out is therapy, wealth, relaxation or tender loving care?
* If this passage was not in the past tense ('you were,' 'you used to' etc) wouldn't it be the most depressing few lines ever written?
* According to this passage, what do all of us deserve?

Episode 3: The Rescue Begins

The Old Testament tells how over many centuries God began to work towards rescuing the human race. He made a promise to a man called Abraham that he was to be the father of a great people, later named Israel, from whom all the nations of the world would be blessed (Genesis 12:1–3 and Genesis 17:3–8). Read **Ephesians 1:4–5 and 2:4–5.**

God could have simply judged and condemned the entire human race. Instead, he chose to act in order to change the situation.

* From these verses what do we learn about God's intentions towards the human race?
* And what do we learn about God's motives for doing this?

In the centuries that followed Abraham, the promises to Israel become clearer. They were to be a special and holy people, a status marked by the practice of male circumcision, and to be separate from the Gentiles – those who were not God's people. To David, the second king of Israel, God made a promise that the blessing would come through a king who would be one of his descendants (2 Samuel 7:8–16). This expected king became known as 'the Anointed One' (in Hebrew Messiah and in Greek Christ). Many prophecies spoke of his coming, for example, Isaiah 9:6–7, Isaiah 11:1–5, Jeremiah 33:15, 20–22 and Micah 5:2.

Read **Ephesians 2:11–12.**

* What, according to these verses, was the situation that the Gentiles were in?
* Because of this, what was the attitude of the Jews towards the Gentiles?

Episode 4: Jesus – the Great Intervention

Finally, the Bible tells of the coming of one of David's descendants, Jesus, who was born of a virgin. Jesus gathered a small group of followers, proclaimed the reign of God and through his teaching and his miracles claimed to be the Son of God. However, instead of being acclaimed king by Israel he was rejected by the people, died on a cross and was buried.

a) Glance through the whole passage of **Ephesians 1:3–2:13**. How many times is the name *Christ* or *Jesus Christ* used? What does this suggest about the importance that Paul gives to him?

b) Look at verses **1:3–8** and **17**. What titles are given to Jesus here? Could these titles have been given to someone who was only human?

c) Read **Ephesians 1:7** and **2:13**.

   + What aspect of Jesus' life is highlighted here?
   + According to these verses, what were the results of Jesus' death for those who believe in him?

Episode 5: The Resurrection: History's Turning Point

The story did not (thankfully!) end with Jesus in the grave. On the third day after his crucifixion he was raised from the dead and on numerous occasions afterwards appeared to his disciples and many hundreds of others. Forty days after the resurrection Jesus ascended into heaven.

Read **Ephesians 1:19** and **2:4–7**.

   + According to these verses, where is Christ now?
   + What is the significance of the resurrection for those who believe in Christ?

Episode 6: The Unfinished Story

Within a few days of Jesus' ascension, the Holy Spirit descended on his followers and the church was born. From then onwards, the good news of Jesus spread rapidly. This episode of the growth and expansion of the church has not yet ended. It is an episode in which we have to play our part.

a) Read **Ephesians 1:5**.

   + What relationship do Jesus' followers now have with God?

b) Read **Ephesians 1:22–23**.

   + What do we learn here about the relationship between Christ and God's new people, the church?

c) Read **Ephesians 1:13–14**.

   + According to this passage, what is the purpose of the Holy Spirit?

Episode 7: The Final Victory

The final episode in the Big Picture is repeatedly mentioned. It is that one day Jesus will return in glory, triumph over evil, judge the human race and bring about God's final and complete reign that will never end.

Read **Ephesians 1:9–10**.

+ If the results of sin were rebellion and breakdown what is the significance of Paul's vision of the future here?

EVALUATION

+ Try and summarise the Big Picture in one, or at the most, two sentences.
+ Who took the initiative to mend the relationship between humankind and God? People? God? Both together?
+ Think about those who are not (or not yet) believers in Christ; what does this passage say about their present relationship to God? Their future?
+ Think about those who are believers in Christ; what does this passage say about their present relationship with God? Their future?
+ Could human beings ever have made themselves right with God?

EXPRESSION

+ How does knowing the Big Picture help us in sharing our faith?
+ According to this passage, what changes does conversion involve?
+ Do we make converts to Christianity or does God make them through us? How do these two very different views affect how we share our faith?
+ The story of God's rescue of a people is unfinished and you and I are part of it. How does this responsibility challenge you?
+ Is your perception of Jesus Christ as big as the Apostle Paul's?
+ Bearing in mind the Big Picture how should Christians view those who are not (yet) believers? The church? The future?

From next week onwards we will be praying for seven people who you know and have contact with and with whom you might be able to share the good news. Over the next week think and pray about choosing the right seven people.

The Building Blocks of Mission: Part 1

Introduction

Christians are people with a message and the point of these studies is to encourage you to explain that message to people in the most effective way possible. However, before examining how we can explain the message most effectively, we need to know what the message is.

You have probably heard the story of the couple travelling through Asia with their much-loved pet dog. In a certain town they found a restaurant and with the aid of gestures and a phrasebook persuaded the waiter to take the dog away and feed him. How they felt when their dog was presented to them, grilled and neatly served up on a plate, can be imagined. They had communicated a message effectively; but it was the wrong message!

In this and the next study I want to look at what I call the building blocks of mission. This is another subject that I covered in more depth in *Calling Out* and in these two studies we will only be able to scratch the surface of what is an important area. These studies will however make the point that we are not just people with a message; we are people with a specific message.

EXPLORATION

In *Calling Out* I suggested that the good news of Jesus could be summarised in terms of six building blocks. These are:

1. God and who he is
2. Sin and the necessity for God to judge it
3. Christ and his substitution for us
4. The gift of the Holy Spirit
5. The implications of making a response
6. The need for a response

This study deals with the first three blocks.

Block 1: God

How do you begin to summarise everything that the Bible has to say about God? Looking at the following passages may, however, help us begin to understand some aspects of who God is.

a) Read **Psalm 102:25–27**.

+ The universe with all its stars, galaxies and planets, appears to be infinitely vast, ancient and permanent. Yet, according to this passage, how is God greater?

b) Read **Exodus 3:1–17**.

This passage is important in understanding the Bible's view of God. The background is that the descendants of Abraham are in slavery in Egypt and a long way from taking possession of the land that was promised to Abraham. Moses has fled from Egypt to the deserts of Sinai.

+ In this meeting between God and Moses who took the initiative? Could we ever find God if he chose not to reveal himself?
+ What characteristic of God is highlighted in verse 5 (and probably hinted at by the presence of fire in verse 2)?
+ God's revelation of his name in verse 14 implies that he is one who is always present and unchanging. This aspect of God's nature underlies the name Yahweh which is translated as the Lord in most English Bibles. Does the idea that God is always present and unchanging encourage or intimidate you?
+ What do we learn from this passage about how the Lord has dealt with Moses' ancestors in the past? What do we learn about his purposes for his people in the future?
+ It has been pointed out that human beings tend to have one of two opposing ideas about God. Some people, especially those influenced by eastern religions, think of God as being cosmic and impersonal, a power or essence which, although awesome and universal, has no personality. Others, especially those influenced by Greek, Roman and Norse mythologies, tend to think of God (or the gods) as limited and personal; he, she or they are little more than super-powerful human beings. What picture do you get here of the God of the Bible?

Block 2: Sin and Judgement

a) Read **Ecclesiastes 7:29**.

This is probably the best short summary of the human condition in the Old Testament.

- What does it tell us about God's intention for the human race?
- What went wrong?
- Who is to blame?

b) In his letter to the Romans the Apostle Paul provides the most thorough and logical discussion of sin in the Bible. Read Romans 1:18–20.

- What, according to this passage, is the reason why human beings are separated from God?
- What is God's reaction to sin?
- People who do not know God's laws might think that they were excused. Are they?

c) Read **Romans 3:23**.

- We tend to think of 'sin' as doing wrong actions, but how does Paul define it here? Does that make it harder or easier to avoid becoming a sinner?
- Who then, is a sinner?
- What sort of person would find it hard to be judged a sinner? What sort of person would find such a verdict easier to accept? Does this explain why Jesus was described as the 'friend of sinners' (Luke 7:34)?

Block 3: Christ and His Substitution

a) Read **Hebrews 1:1–3**.

- What, according to verse 1, was the task of the Old Testament prophets?
- How is Jesus similar to these people? How is he different?

Now read **Hebrews 1:8–12**.

- Verses 10–12 quote those verses in Psalm 102 which we looked at earlier. In the Psalm who did these words apply to? Who does the writer to the Hebrews say that they apply to here?
- So what is he saying about Jesus?

b) Read **Romans 3:23–26**.

Underlying this famous passage are two concepts: God's justice and his love.

- According to God's justice what ought to be everybody's fate?
- Why did Jesus need to come? Couldn't God just forgive people?
- What, according to this passage, are some of the things that Jesus has done to rescue us?
- How, according to this passage, do we take hold of the forgiveness offered to us in Jesus?

EVALUATION

Do as many of these questions as you can.

a) Think about the phrase 'God loves you'. Is it:

- An *accurate* statement of the good news of Jesus?
- An *adequate* statement of the good news of Jesus?

b) Imagine the following people. Which of the three building blocks that you have looked at might give them a problem?

- Someone who believes that Jesus was just a good man.
- Someone who believes that God is all-loving and can forgive 'just like that'.
- Someone who believes that human beings are basically good.
- Someone who believes that God is merely a force.

c) Think of the people you are most likely to be able to share Jesus with – relatives, neighbours, friends, colleagues at work. Which of these three building blocks is:

- The one that you think they least want to hear?
- The one that they most need to know about?
- The one you feel least comfortable talking about?
- What can you do about any of these weaknesses?

d) Imagine that you are talking with the following people. What links might you find in order to talk to them about God, sin and judgement, Christ and his substitution?

- A middle-aged man wanders into the church building because he has been inspired by classical music and is seeking to find out about the source of creativity and beauty.

• A retired woman comes to church because she has suffered a great tragedy in her family. Lonely and scared, she thinks she has wasted her life.
• A distant cousin who is enthusiastic about an art exhibition on the life of Jesus and who wants to find out more about Christianity.
• A young couple at a friend's house who are fascinated by ideas about eternal life. They watch a lot of films.
• A group of teenagers who have a passionate sense of justice and are very active in seeking fair trade and human rights.
• A friend from work who, as a single parent, wants you to help her organise a small ceremony to bless her newborn child.

e) Imagine you are talking to the following people about Christianity:

• Someone who believes that God and the Devil are the same.
• Someone who believes that God is a force and not a person.
• Someone who believes in God but doesn't believe that he can be a God of love.

In each case do you try and clear away the misconception or ignore it and hope that, when they get converted, it will eventually sort itself out?

f) The three building blocks here have been given in a logical order, 1. God the creator, 2. the human problem and 3. Jesus, God's solution. However, is this order the only way of telling the story? Think of the following people:

• Someone who is grieving over the recent death of their wife or husband.
• Someone who is guilt-ridden over the failure of a relationship.
• A seven-year old child in hospital, who is scared of dying.

Would you tell the good news in the same way to each of them? How might you modify it?

EXPRESSION

a) If you know each other quite well as a group, the following exercise might be helpful.

Cut up enough small slips of paper so that everybody in the group has one for each person. Ask them to write the name of a group participant on a slip of paper and underneath, in no more than a few words or a sentence, the gifts that they think that this person has in communicating or talking to people about Jesus. They should do this for all the members of the group. Next, pass round envelopes marked with the names of all the group members. The slips are put into the appropriate envelope without anyone else seeing what has been written. At the end of the study the envelopes are given to the individuals for them to look at privately and think about at their leisure. As we are all very sceptical about how God can possibly use us in reaching out to others, this can be a great source of encouragement and a good way of building each other up.

b) Think of situations during the past week where you have encountered people who needed to know the good news of Jesus. How did you do in terms of sharing your faith ? How could you have done better? Pray that you would have opportunities in the coming week to be faithful to the good news.

c) Remember the seven people that you were going to pray about? Get together with one or more members of the group and pray together for those that you have named on your list. We will be thinking about them each week.

d) As part of a closing time of prayer think of those groups or individuals you know who are in the 'front line' of telling people about Jesus. Is there anything more that God is calling you to do for them – pray, call, meet up or write a letter?

The Building Blocks of Mission: Part 2

Introduction

Consider the following 'famous last words':

+ 'It's really quite safe to hold the red wire: look . . .'
+ 'Do you really think I would be holding this if it was a live grenade?'
+ 'Of course there's no train coming . . .'
+ 'I'm telling you, those warnings about dangerous cliffs are only there for legal reasons . . .'
+ 'Actually, they are really quite friendly when they have been fed. You can even stroke them. Just like this. . . .'

In all these cases the decision was a mistake based on faulty or inadequate information; there was something the 'shortly-to-be-deceased' had over-looked.

In sharing the good news of Jesus it is important that we do not miss anything out. In the previous study we covered the first three of the building blocks (God, sin and judgement, and Christ and his substitution for us). In this study, I want to cover the second three blocks – the gift of the Holy Spirit, the implications of making a response and the need for a response.

Taken together these six components give the basic framework of the good news; miss out one or more and there is a danger that what we have is no longer really God's good news – it is something else.

EXPLORATION

The three parts of this section correspond to the final three 'building blocks' of the good news.

Block 4: The Gift of the Holy Spirit

a) In the Old Testament the Spirit is seen as the 'breath' of the Lord and the agent through which he works. In fact 'breath' and 'spirit' are the same word in Hebrew (and Greek). Share out the following short passages from the Old Testament among the group. After each one is read out, discuss what it tells us about who God's Spirit is and what he does.

Read **Genesis 1:1–2; Psalm 33:6; 1 Samuel 16:13; Judges 6:34–35; Micah 3:8** (*Note: this is the prophet Micah speaking.*) **Isaiah 61:1** (*Note: The speaker here is assumed to be the coming Messiah.*)

b) The New Testament talks much more about the Holy Spirit.

(i) Luke, the writer of both the gospel that bears his name and its sequel, the book of Acts, was very interested in the Holy Spirit. Look at the following brief passages from the start of Luke's gospel.

Read **Luke 3:21–22; Luke 3:15–16; Luke 4:1; Luke 4:16–20.**

From these verses how is the Holy Spirit important in

- ✦ empowering Jesus?
- ✦ guiding Jesus?
- ✦ confirming who Jesus was?

(ii) On the night before his crucifixion Jesus talked to his disciples about the Holy Spirit; his teaching on this subject is recorded in John.

Read **John 14:15–17, 26.**

What is the relationship between the Counsellor and Christ? Note verse 17.

- ✦ Why do the disciples need another Counsellor (verse 16)?
- ✦ What things will the Counsellor do for Christ's people?
- ✦ Is this still his role today?

Block 5: The Implications of Making a Response

The good news is that Jesus loves us and wants to have a relationship with us. However, the only relationship he will allow is one that is exclusive and based on a total commitment to him.

a) Read **Joshua 24:14–15.**

This is Joshua's farewell address to the Israelites in his old age.

- ◆ What danger is Joshua addressing here?
- ◆ What is the challenge to the Israelites? Does God make a similar challenge to those wanting to follow him today?
- ◆ What would it mean to put away our idols in today's culture?

b) Read **Luke 14:25–33**.

How does verse 25 explain why Jesus gave such stern teaching?

- ◆ According to this passage what must not get in the way of following Jesus? What other things might you add to this?
- ◆ What do the two short parables in this passage mean? Explain in your own words.

Block 6: The Need for a Response

The entire Bible is a call to commitment; there has to be a response. We may persuade people to admire Jesus' teaching but admiration is not enough. Only a total following and a wholehearted commitment is adequate.

a) The call to choose occurs in many places in the Old Testament.

Read **Deuteronomy 30:19–20**.

- ◆ Summarise the two options that Moses offers the Israelites here.

b) Read **Galatians 2:20**.

- ◆ How many times do the words 'I', 'me' or 'my' occur in this famous summary of what the good news is all about? How would you describe the way that Paul had taken hold of the message of Jesus?
- ◆ Can you apply this text personally to yourself?

EVALUATION

a) The Greek word Jesus uses for the Holy Spirit in John 14 is *parakletos*, which basically means 'someone called alongside'. Various words have been used to try to translate this into English: *advocate* (or defence lawyer), *strengthener, encourager, counsellor, guide* are all possible translations and all convey something of the role of the Spirit.

- How was Jesus an advocate, strengthener, encourager, counsellor and guide to his disciples when he was on earth?
- How is the Holy Spirit an advocate, strengthener, encourager, counsellor and guide to Jesus' followers today?

b) What might the cost of following Jesus be for the following people:

- A business executive whose boss expects total commitment to the company.
- A young woman from another religion whose father has said he will consider her as being dead if she becomes a believer in Jesus.
- A man who defrauded his company of £500 ten years ago in a crime that has been undetected.
- A man who has not spoken to his mother since a blazing row five years ago.
- A woman who, with some friends, has a home decorating business that, in order to avoid tax, only accepts cash payments.
- A woman who is living with her boyfriend.

How can Christians help new believers deal with the consequences of becoming a follower of Jesus?

c) Why do people delay in making a decision to follow Jesus? Are some delays legitimate? What are the dangers of pushing people into a commitment that they are not ready for?

d) Imagine that you are faced with two people who are thinking about becoming Christians.

- One person comes from a really difficult background and feels daunted by the idea of living the Christian life. What encouragement might you offer them?
- The other person is already living according to a high moral standard. They seem to think that the Christian lifestyle is something that they can easily manage. What would you say to them?

EXPRESSION

a) What situations might you face this week in which you can put into practice some of the truths you have learnt here?

b) Do we tend to avoid telling people what the cost to them of following Jesus might be? Why?

c) Many of us present the good news of Jesus as something that people can either take or leave. Should there be more urgency?

d) Pray for those you know who do the work of evangelists. Try and find information about their work so you can pray for them more effectively. Please include me!

e) Consider the seven people you have on your prayer list. Is there anything new to report? Join with other members of your group to pray together for those you have named.

Why We Should Call Out . . . And Why We Don't

Introduction

In this study we will look at two sides of the same coin: why we should share our faith and why we tend not to. I should say that in *Calling Out* I spend two chapters looking at these issues and by no means exhausted the matter. This is only really an overview of a big subject. Nevertheless, I hope it will encourage you to share your faith more effectively.

EXPLORATION

This is in two parts. First, we will look at the reasons for sharing our faith and then we will look at some reasons why we don't tend to do it very often.

1. Why we should share our faith

In *Calling Out* I suggested five reasons why we had to tell people about Jesus:

- As Christians we should have a *compulsion* to tell them.
- We have been *commanded* to tell them.
- We are *convinced* that people need to hear about Jesus.
- We have *compassion* for people who have not heard about Jesus.
- The church was *created* to tell people about Jesus.

Here, I want to treat them together.

a) Who calls out to those who are not Christians? Is it the responsibility of all Christians or just of a group of specialists?

(i) Read **1 Peter 3:15–16**.

Peter's first letter is directed to ordinary Christians in churches spread across what today is Turkey.

- What is Peter urging in verse 15b? What alternatives are there to 'being ready to explain' your Christian hope?
- If you are being 'asked about your Christian hope' who is taking the initiative? Why does this make sharing your faith easier? How can we live lives that arouse a genuine interest in our faith?
- Verse 16a gives advice on the manner in which the truth is to be shared. How might our witness to Jesus not be done with gentleness and respect?

(ii) Although the Bible makes it plain that all Christians are called to engage in evangelism and be witnesses to what God has done for them in Jesus, it also indicates that there are those Christians whom God has specifically called and gifted to be evangelists.

Read **Ephesians 4:11–13**.

- Briefly, how would you define the various job descriptions of the different ministries listed in verse 11?
- What, according to verses 12 and 13, should be the goal of their work?
- Which of these gifts do you think God has given you?
- Which of these gifts do others think God has given you?

b) Read **2 Corinthians 5:11–6:2**.

The background to this passage is that false teachers have infiltrated the young church in Corinth. These people have cast doubts on Paul's motives, his ability and his authority to be an apostle.

- If you only had this passage of the Bible, what could you learn about the message of the good news? (see verses 15–19, 21). Try to use your own words.
- What do we learn from this passage about the position of those who have not yet responded to the message of Jesus? See verses 14b, 18, 19, 21 – and notice Paul's urgency in verses 20 and 6:1. If the message of Jesus is called the good news, why is this the 'bad news'?
- On the basis of this passage how would you describe the manner in which Paul did his work? See verses 11,13 and 20. You may also want to glance down at 6:3–10.
- What motivates this enthusiasm? (See verses 11,13,14,18,20.)

- What is Paul's attitude towards the fact that God has called him to be a messenger of the good news? Tolerant acceptance of his lot? Grumbling? (See verses 19, 6:1.)
- Paul repeatedly defends his motives (verses 11b,12). What wrong motives for witness does he mention?
- From this passage, what impression do you get of the sort of person Paul was?
- Could you rewrite this passage in the first person singular, using *I*, *my* and *me* rather than *we*, *our* and *us*? How does this passage challenge us in the area of how we witness to Jesus?

c) For most of his ministry, Jesus urged his followers to keep silent about who he was. All this changed after the resurrection.

(i) Read **John 20:19–21**.

- Think about the phrase, 'As the Father has sent me, so I send you'.
- What were God's motives in Jesus coming to earth? How are they similar to our motives for mission?
- What was the cost to Jesus of his mission? What should that say to us about our expectations for mission?
- It is not just Jesus speaking here, but Jesus risen from the dead. How does that affect a) the importance and b) the authority of this 'sending out'?
- The pattern here is that God sends people to call out. What difference does it make that our 'calling out' is the result of God 'sending us out' first? Is this an encouragement or a challenge?

(ii) Read **Matthew 28:16–20**.

Verses 19 and 20 are very well known but we mustn't ignore verse 18!

- Here Jesus is sending out the disciples to proclaim the good news to the ends of the earth. What is the relevance to this task of him saying that he has been given 'complete authority'?
- What difference would it make to our sharing the good news of Jesus out if he hadn't been given such authority?

Look at verses 19 and 20a. Here Jesus is explaining exactly what the disciples are to do and where they are to do it. In your own words answer the following:

- What are to be their objectives?
- Where are they to do this?

- How are they to do this?
- What do you see as the significance of the instruction to baptise new followers?

Finally, look at verse 20b.

- What is Jesus promising?
- Why is it appropriate in the context of being 'sent out to call out'?
- How do you think the disciples felt when they heard this promise? How should we feel about this promise?

2. And why we don't!

In *Calling Out* I suggested that there are a number of reasons why people don't share their faith with others. Here we can only look at a few.

a) One of the best pictures in the Bible of someone who was totally committed to 'calling out' for God under even the most difficult circumstances is the Old Testament prophet Jeremiah. For forty years he proclaimed God's word to the southern kingdom of Judah surviving abuse, threats, murder attempts, imprisonments and invasion. Jeremiah's message consisted almost entirely of bad news. God, he announced, was going to severely judge his people. But Jeremiah was no super-hero.

Read **Jeremiah 1:1–10; 17–19**.

- According to verses 4 and 10 what is the mission that God says Jeremiah has been appointed to?
- What is Jeremiah's response to God in verse 6? From God's words in verses 8 and 17 what do you think were the underlying issues? Can you sympathise?
- List the specific encouragements that God offers Jeremiah (see verses 5, 7, 9, 10, 18, 19). If God gave you these encouragements would they help you be a better witness for him?

b) Now read **Luke 12:4–12**.

Here Jesus seems to be teaching a group of people that included both those who were committed to him as well as those who were, as yet, uncommitted.

Jesus is not just referring to his followers, his 'friends' (see verse 4) witnessing for him in situations that are unwelcoming, but to being witnesses for him in situations where their very lives would be at stake. While few of us might face this sort of extreme challenge today, the principles Jesus set out apply in every situation where we have an opportunity to speak out for Jesus.

+ According to verses 4 and 5 what is one antidote to being afraid of people? What does it mean for one of Jesus' 'friends' (verse 4; see John 15:15) to fear God?
+ What specific concern do you think Jesus is addressing in verses 6 and 7? What point do the references to sparrows and birds make?
+ In verse 8 Jesus says the issue is whether we acknowledge him publicly. What would it have meant for his hearers to have acknowledged him publicly? What does it mean for us? How is verse 8 an encouragement to Jesus' faithful followers? And how is verse 9 a warning to the uncommitted?

Look at verses 11 and 12.

+ What is the situation that verse 11 talks about? (See Acts 22:19 for an example). What would be the nearest equivalent in today's society to this sort of situation?
+ What specific fear is addressed in verses 11 and 12?
+ What answer to that fear does Jesus promise? (See John 14:26; Acts 1:8):
+ What in this passage challenges you about how you do not share your faith?
+ When looking at Jeremiah in the previous study passage, we read about the many promises that God made to him. Are the promises given to us here as great? How ought this passage encourage us to call out with more boldness?

EVALUATION

+ List the reasons for sharing your faith in Jesus that have emerged in the course of this study. Which seem the most compelling to you?
+ List some of the difficulties in 'calling out' that you have touched on. What gifts and help has God provided to help you overcome these difficulties?

EXPRESSION

a) Sometimes we have to make an instant response. Pick a few of the following and think about how you would give an instant response in these situations.

+ It is your first day at a new job and over coffee the group of people you work with are talking about last night's TV. One of them says there was something on about 'some weird church'. Another turns to you and asks, 'Are you religious?'
+ You are visiting a non-Christian friend of yours who you have known for years. They look at you and say, 'Do you think I'm going to hell?'

- You are on a time away exercise with work colleagues. Your boss turns to you and says, 'I want you to talk for five minutes to us all about the really important things in your life.'
- Someone asks you to countersign a forged claim for expenses. You refuse and, in a rather irritated way, they turn to you and say, 'Why won't you help me?'
- You go round to see your neighbour. Full of grief they tell you about a close young relative who has just died after a long and debilitating illness. They look at you and ask, "Why did God let it happen?"

Having thought about what you would say, now ask the following questions:

- What is the worst possible outcome in these situations?
- Is this worst-case scenario actually likely to happen?
- Are our fears about sharing our faith based on reality or fantasy?

b) Is sharing the good news of Jesus something that is top of the agenda in (i) your life, (ii) the life of your church?

c) Go back to the names of the seven people you have on your prayer list. Is there anything new to report? Get together with other members of the group and pray for those you have named.

The 'Where' of Mission – Sharing Our Faith Here, There and Everywhere

Introduction

Jesus' last earthly words to the disciples included this promise in **Acts 1:8**:

But when the Holy Spirit has come upon you, you will receive power and will tell people about me everywhere – in Jerusalem, throughout Judea, in Samaria, and to the ends of the earth.

This promise (or is it an order?) sets the pattern for the spread of the early church as shown in the book of Acts where the focus is in Jerusalem (chapters 1–7), Judea and Samaria (chapters 8–12) and the 'ends of the earth' (from chapter 13 onwards).

I believe this gradual expansion of the disciples' witness to Jesus is not just a fact of church history but is also a helpful pattern for the way we share the good news with people. I think all of us can identify four zones for witness:

- A 'Jerusalem zone', which is our inner circle of friends and family.
- A 'Judea zone', which is made up of our neighbours and colleagues.
- A 'Samaria zone', which is made up of people who we connect with but who we don't necessarily get on well with.
- An 'ends of the earth zone', which is everybody else.

In this study we will go through these four zones.

EXPLORATION

The background

Let's look at that key passage at the start of Acts.

Read **Acts 1:6–11**.

The question the disciples raise in verse 6 tells us a lot about the things that, even after forty days with the risen Jesus, they were still focused on.

◆ What sort of kingdom were they thinking about?
◆ What was the geographical limit of their hopes?
◆ What attitude to non-Jews is implied by their question?
◆ Why do you think Jesus doesn't answer their question? Are there lessons for us in his refusal to answer?
◆ Ten days later when the Spirit came on the disciples with power, the meaning of this command must have been clearer. But what do you suppose they thought about it in the meantime?
◆ Are we ever guilty of having limited horizons?

We will look further at the role of the Spirit in witnessing in Study 7. However for the moment, think about the following question: How do the disciples in the latter part of the book of Acts differ from the people portrayed here?

1. To Jerusalem: our inner circle

a) Jesus commanded the disciples to share the good news in Jerusalem first of all.

Read **Psalm 132:13–14; Isaiah 2:2–3; Psalm 137:1–6**.

◆ Imagine you were a faithful Jew in Jesus' day. When you thought of Jerusalem what would come to mind?
◆ What personal memories would Jerusalem have had for the disciples? What was their own 'track-record' in Jerusalem?

Read **Mark 14:50** and **70–72**.

b) We can think of our lives as having a 'Jerusalem zone' – our inner circle of friends and family. It need not involve people who are geographically close; after all, someone whom you work with or whom you email regularly on the other side of the world might fit in this zone.

◆ What is easy about sharing your faith within the 'Jerusalem zone'?
◆ What is hard about the 'Jerusalem zone'?

Read **Mark 3:20–21; Matthew 13:53–58**.

◆ Can you avoid sharing your faith in your 'Jerusalem zone'? What would people think about someone who was 'on fire' for Jesus when they went abroad but was merely 'a flickering flame' amongst their friends and colleagues?

2. To Judea: the neighbourly neighbours

Judea was the part of Israel around Jerusalem.

a) It is worthwhile looking at how the good news reached Judea.

Read **Acts 6:7**.

Priests worked in the temple on a rotating basis and so some of these converts had probably come up to Jerusalem from the Judean countryside to perform their share of the temple duties.

- ◆ What things would people in Judea have had in common with those in Jerusalem?
- ◆ On the basis of what is said (or not said) here, how do you think that the gospel spread into Judea?
- ◆ Have you known situations in which the good news spread 'naturally' without any human strategy? What is good about this way of sharing the good news? What are the limits of this sort of unplanned evangelism?

Now read **Acts 8:1b–4** which tells what happened after Stephen was martyred.

- ◆ What happened to the church in Jerusalem?
- ◆ If you had been forced to flee from somewhere because persecution of Christians was taking place, what attitude towards witnessing would you be tempted to take in your new place of residence? How did these Christians react?
- ◆ What lessons do we learn here about how God can use evil events for his purposes?

b) We can think of our lives as having a 'Judea zone'; a circle of contacts with whom we have a similar language and culture but who we do not know particularly well.

- ◆ What are the positive aspects of sharing Jesus within your 'Judea zone'?
- ◆ What are the negative aspects?

3. To Samaria: the not-so-neighbourly neighbours

Samaria, where the Samaritans lived, lay to the north of Judea and broadly covered the area of the Old Testament kingdom of Israel. Over centuries the Samaritans had separated from the Jews; they had intermarried with Gentiles, only accepted the first five books of the Old Testament and felt that the holy site for worship was not Jerusalem, but their own Mount Gerizim. Although there were enormous similarities between the two communities there were major racial, religious, cultural and political differences. The result was a long and well-remembered history of insults and violence between the communities. In fact Jews travelling from Galilee to Judea would make a long detour across the Jordan just to avoid Samaria.

a) Let's look at the background to Samaria and the Samaritans.

(i) Read **Luke 9:51–56**.

- What do we learn here of the disciples' attitude to their Samaritan neighbours?
- What situations do you know of today where this sort of loathing exists between cultural and ethnic groups?

(ii) Read **Acts 8:4–8; 14–17**.

- Who had been persecuting the church? So why was Philip able to be so bold in Samaria?
- The hostile division between the Samaritans and the Jews had gone on for centuries. What action was taken by the church leaders to ensure this division was not carried over into the early church? What lessons are there here for how we deal with converts from groups or cultures that are in dispute with one another?

b) We can think of our lives as having a 'Samaria zone'; a circle of contacts with whom we have some similarities but from whom we are also separated. Sadly, this may include people at our place of work or even within our families.

- Give examples of people with whom you could have strong links, but for the fact that any bridges to them have been broken. (Be sensitive when recounting personal experiences.)
- What are the difficulties in sharing Jesus with people in the 'Samaria zone'?
- What principles or ideas can you think of to try to build (or rebuild) bridges to people in this category?

4. To the ends of the earth: no one is excluded

The final zone is the 'ends of the earth', which is everybody else, however distant or remote. With these people, the only links we may have are our shared humanity and the fact that they too need to hear the good news of Jesus.

To the Jews 'the ends of the earth' wasn't just a phrase that meant distance, it meant *Gentiles*. In Jesus' time Jewish thinking was dominated by the idea of being pure and separate and as a result Gentiles were, if at all possible, to be avoided.

a) The book of Acts not only shows the deep-seated problems Jews had with Gentiles, but also the extraordinary way in which the gap between the two was bridged in the church. The classic account is the conversion of Cornelius in Acts 10. A brief summary of what happened is as follows. Through an angel, God tells Cornelius, a Roman army officer based at Caesarea, to send men to find Peter and bring him back. While they are on their journey, Peter has a vision in which God tells him to eat animals that are unclean under Jewish law.

Read **Acts 10:24–11:4**.

+ What do we learn about the attitude of the Jews towards the Gentiles here (Acts 10:28; 11:2–3)?
+ How many miracles/signs/extraordinary events are described in Acts 10:1–44? What does this suggest about the size of the gulf between Jew and Gentile that had to be bridged?
+ Look at Peter's message about Jesus in verses 36–43. What are the main elements in it?
+ Although their religious beliefs varied, Romans generally greatly feared the supernatural world and felt that it was vital to keep the peace with the gods. As a race that ruled much of the known world they also understood and valued the idea of power and authority. What is present in this message that might be appropriate to someone from such a background?
+ What is omitted from this message that might be distracting or irrelevant to someone from such a background?

What lessons are here for us about

+ who we share the good news with?
+ how we share the good news with them?

b) The short Old Testament book of Jonah tells the story of a very reluctant missionary.

(i) Read **Jonah 1:1–3**.

Nineveh was the capital of the cruel Assyrians, the great empire to the east of Israel; Tarshish was probably in Spain, which was popularly believed to mark the western end of the world.

- Why do you think Jonah decided to run away to the opposite 'end of the earth'?
- How does this escape plan show that Jonah had an incorrect perception of God's power?
- Do we ever run away from God's calling to witness?

As the rest of Jonah 1 and 2 point out, the result is disastrous. Jonah is swallowed by a great fish and ends up being spat out back onto land.

(ii) Read **Jonah 3 and 4**.

- When Jonah finally does go to Nineveh what reception does his message get? How does God respond to the repentance of Nineveh?
- Why isn't Jonah happy about this turn of events? What does this reveal about Jonah's real motives for fleeing westwards?
- How does this show that Jonah not only had an incorrect perception of God's power but also of his character?
- What do we learn about God's character from these verses?
- Successful preaching of the good news to our enemies means that God will have mercy on them and bless them. Is that something that we really want? Be honest!

(iii) In the New Testament Paul's attitude to mission is very different from that of Jonah.

Read **Romans 15:14–24**.

- The letter to the Romans was probably written around AD 57–59 which would mean that Paul would have been preaching for around a quarter of century and was, in all probability, nearly sixty. A recent book1 comments that, in Rome at this time, 'average life expectancy is generally agreed to have been about twenty-five years.' Do you see any evidence of Paul slowing down?
- Illyricum was the Roman province that covered the Balkans. From a map or a Bible atlas, find out how far it is from Jerusalem. Where does Paul want to go to now? How does this compare with Jonah's desire to go to the same place?
- What drives Paul on? Have you met people with a similar motivation?

EVALUATION

a) How would you define the 'Jerusalem zone' for an individual? For a church?

- Do you share the good news of Jesus in your personal 'Jerusalem zone'?
- Why is it sometimes easy to give up with this zone?
- What contact have you had with people in this zone during the last week? What contacts are you likely to have with them this week?
- With respect to your church, where does your Jerusalem zone lie? Are you involved in sharing the good news there?

b) How would you define the 'Judea zone' for an individual? For a church?

- Who is in your 'Judea zone'?
- What contact have you had with people in this zone over the past week where the good news of Jesus might have surfaced? What contacts will you have with them next week? Are you prepared to share the love of God in Jesus to them?
- What do you think is the most effective form of reaching out to this group? Why?
- Is your church involved in evangelism in its 'Judea zone'? What things might be effective? What might be inappropriate?

c) How would you define the 'Samaria zone' for an individual? For a church?

- Who is in your 'Samaria' zone?
- Do you go out of your way to meet the 'Samaritans' in your life? How can you meet them?
- What is the divide between you and them? How can you bridge it?
- Who, in your community represent Samaritans? How can your church get involved with them?

d) How would you define the 'ends of the earth zone' for an individual? For a church?

- What is your attitude towards the 'ends of the earth zone'? Is it a personal challenge or is it something that you think is for other people?
- What can you do to get involved in reaching those in the ends of the earth zone? How can your church get more involved in this?

EXPRESSION

a) Look again at **Acts 1:8**.

How do you view this statement?

- Is it Jesus' instructions for his first followers and, as such, a fascinating piece of church history? (*Polite yawn.*)
- Is it Jesus' instructions to me personally for my life? (*Gulp!*)

b) Think about these four areas and privately give yourself marks out of five for each area. Where are you weakest? What can you do about it? What deters you from a more effective witness for Jesus? What can you do to remedy this?

c) People who are serious financial investors often have a portfolio of investments in different ventures. Why not have a 'mission portfolio' of interests in each of the four zones?

d) How can you help support those full-time workers in difficult areas who are attempting to spread the good news of Jesus? Can you pray for them? Can you support them? Can you write to them to show your support of their ministry?

e) When eighteenth and nineteenth century missionaries left for countries like China and India they were not expected to return alive. Sometimes it took a year for news of their arrival to make it back to their home church. Nowadays you can get almost anywhere in the world in twenty-four hours; instant global phone or internet communication networks extend almost worldwide, and the life expectancy of missionaries is not much worse than anyone else in a church. But why has the western church lost interest in reaching out to the ends of the earth? What can you do to revive its interest in this vital area? (How about reading some good books? Going on a mission conference? Having a missionary evening at your church?)

f) We often long for the power of the Holy Spirit to descend on our churches as it did on the early church. But do we also long to have the same extraordinary vision and zeal to go across all barriers and reach others for Christ?

- Pray that your personal witness will be inspired and empowered by the Spirit.
- Pray that you will be led by the Spirit to act and to speak for him.
- Pray that you will get opportunities to speak for him.
- Pray that the Spirit will continue his work of spreading the good news throughout the earth through organisations, projects and individuals.

g) Go to the names of the seven people you have on your prayer list. Is there anything more recent to report? Get together with other members of the group and pray for those you have named together.

The Seven Pillars of Mission: Part 1 – Prayer, Presence, Proclamation

Introduction

In the final two studies we will look at those things that are essential for us to do in order to share Jesus effectively with other people. In *Calling Out* I called these things the Seven Pillars of Mission and identified the first three pillars as follows:

- Prayer – all that we do must be rooted in God and his will and power.
- Presence – we can only speak to people about Jesus if we are with them.
- Proclamation – we must speak out about Jesus.

EXPLORATION

Prayer

a) The Bible makes it plain that Jesus is not merely the person at the heart of our message; he is also the example of what it is to be a messenger of the good news.

Read out the following passages: **Luke 3:21–22; Mark 1:35–38; Luke 5:15–16; Luke 6:12–13; Luke 9:18; Luke 22:39–46**

- Notice how we are told that Jesus prayed at critical times of his ministry – at his baptism, before calling the disciples, before Peter's declaration that Jesus is the Messiah and finally before the crucifixion. What does this suggest?
- Did Jesus only pray at times of crisis?
- What do we learn about the way Jesus prayed?
- What lessons should we draw from the fact that Jesus prayed so frequently?

b) Read **Ephesians 6:10–20**.

- How does Paul describe the Christian life here?
- What do we learn about the forces that oppose us?
- What is the role of prayer in this spiritual warfare (see verse 18)?
- In verses 19–20 Paul asks that the church pray for him as he shares Jesus with other people. How does this relate to the previous verses?
- What are his specific requests?
- What lessons are there here for how we should personally share our faith?
- What lessons are there for how we support others who are full-time evangelists and missionaries?

c) Read **2 Corinthians 4:3–6** and **Ephesians 2:1–6**.

- How does Paul describe the state of those who are not believers in Jesus Christ?
- What does this say about what happens when people are converted?
- Why, on the basis of these passages, would you say that prayer is an essential part of sharing our faith?

Presence

a) Normally we need to be present with someone to effectively share Jesus with them. Jesus himself gives the supreme example of 'presence' in sharing God's good news.

Read **John 1:1–18**.

- From this passage what do you understand by 'the Word'? How does this describe what Jesus is?
- What is the relationship of the Word to God and to the world?
- What reaction did the Word receive when he came to earth?
- What principle of mission does Jesus set out here?

Now read **John 3:16–17**.

- From both passages try to summarise why Jesus came.

b) For God to have come to earth as a wealthy, privileged human being would have been awesome enough. But in Jesus, God went even further.

Read **John 13:1–17**.

- Who would have washed people's feet in Jesus' day? Who would never ever have done it?

- According to verse 1 what motivated Jesus?
- What does Jesus' dramatic illustration say about himself? What can we learn from it?
- Most churches believe that Jesus is teaching that we should obey the principle of foot washing rather than literally practising it. Come up with some examples of how a church or an individual Christian might carry out this principle. How might this relate to witnessing about Jesus?

Proclamation

a) At the end of Luke's Gospel we read how the risen Jesus gave his followers some commands.

Read **Luke 24:44–48**.

In verses 44–46 Jesus refers to the Old Testament.

- What claim does he make about himself?
- Why is the witness of the Old Testament an important part of any proclamation about Jesus?
- In verses 47–48 Jesus gives the disciples the message they are to take.
- What does the message promise? On what conditions?
- To whom is it to be sent?
- What does it mean for Jesus to give the disciples his authority?
- What other help does he promise?

b) Read **Romans 10:8–15**.

- What according to verses 8–13 is needed for someone to be saved?
- What, according to verses 14–15, is the responsibility that is placed on those of us who already know about Jesus?

EVALUATION

Answer as many of these questions as you can.

Prayer

- Ultimately who is responsible for people becoming Christians? Why then is prayer so important?
- What are we saying to God when we engage in sharing our faith without having prayed about it first?

+ What other reasons can you give for why prayer is vital to sharing our faith?
+ If we really believed that our prayers changed things, how would it make a difference to the way we prayed?
+ In terms of your witness what would be the bravest prayer you could pray?

Presence

+ When do actions speak louder than words? When can our actions contradict the words we speak? Can you think of any first-hand instances of this?
+ Why do people tend to listen more carefully to people they know than they do to strangers? Why is 'being there' important?
+ In the book of Acts the Christians went out into the world to share the good news; in contrast we tend to expect people to come to church to hear it. How can (or should) we adopt the strategy of the early church?
+ What strikes you most about the way that Jesus was present in the world?
+ While we may agree that 'being there' is a great idea why do we tend to opt out and stand back?
+ If your church ceased to exist, would it make any difference to the surrounding area or community?

Proclamation

+ Why do we tend to think that proclaiming Jesus is someone else's job?
+ Do we ever find ourselves slipping into the frame of mind where we think, 'If only my friends or family could hear so-and-so speak, they might become Christians'? What is that saying about how we see ourselves?
+ How do we justify ourselves when we fail to proclaim Jesus? Are these excuses valid?
+ Do we always proclaim Christianity as good news? Or does the 'good' element of it sometimes get removed?

EXPRESSION

William Temple, a twentieth-century Archbishop of Canterbury, once said, 'The church is the only organisation which exists for the benefit of its non-members.'

+ Do you agree?
+ Could your church adopt this as its motto?
+ Is getting the good news to unbelievers a priority for you? For your church?

Prayer

- Do you believe that prayer is vital for your witness to be effective? Do you practise that belief? How can you motivate yourself to pray?
- Think about a particular time when you prayed specifically for a person or a situation and you were surprised by the outcome of your prayers. Encourage each other with brief stories of prayers for people that were answered.
- Is our praying directed to specific people or places or is it vague and all-purpose – 'Bless the neighbourhood . . .' ?
- Why not examine what you pray for? How much of your time is spent praying for others? How much time is spent praying for people to come to faith in Christ?
- If you could make just one change to help your pattern of praying, what would that change be? How could you take a step towards that?

Presence

- Why is it easier to be with Christians than people who don't go to church? How can we avoid creating Christian 'ghettos' or cliques?
- Where do you have 'a presence'? At work? In your community? How many hours a week do you spend in a situation where you might be able to talk about Jesus to people who do not know him?
- What might you do to get more involved in your community? Can you get involved in a non-church activity in your area, like the neighbourhood watch, a PTA association, an environmental organisation or being a school governor? Are you too involved in church activities to connect with the unchurched?
- What things does your community struggle with? What issues are there in your community that no one wants to deal with? How, in the spirit of John 13:1–17, can you get involved?
- What could you do with your leisure time in order to have more contact with non-Christians?

Imagine that Jesus were to come to your community:

- Where might he go?
- Who might he mix with? What leads you to suggest that?
- Are there Christians who are found in these areas? If not, why not?
- Are we prepared to take the risk of moving out of our comfort zone? Are we prepared to be rejected?

Proclamation

- If someone came to you and asked what it meant to be a Christian what things could you say?
- Are you an invisible Christian? Do invisible Christians have an invisible message?
- What situations might you face this week in which you can put into practice some of the truths that you have learnt together?
- Return to the names of the seven people on your prayer list for the past five weeks. Is there anything to report? Continue to pray for them.

The Seven Pillars of Mission: Part 2 – Persuasion, Power, Praise, Patterning

Introduction

In the introduction to Study 6, I identified seven elements which are essential in order to share Jesus effectively with other people. We then looked briefly at the first three of these 'Seven Pillars of Mission': prayer, presence and proclamation. In this study we will look at four more pillars. These are:

- Persuasion – to speak with people to help them understand the truth of the good news.
- Power – to allow the Holy Spirit to work in the way he chooses.
- Praise – to honour God in all that we do and make sure that all the glory is given back to him.
- Patterning – to ensure new believers become disciples.

EXPLORATION

Persuasion

a) Read **Acts 13:13–42**.

Paul is preaching here to Jews and Gentiles who were sympathetic to the Jewish faith in Pisidian Antioch in what is now central Turkey. Presumably Paul spoke longer than this and what Luke has recorded is the summary of what was said. How does Paul build bridges with this particular audience by:

- where he goes to meet them?
- the quotations that he uses?
- the nature of his argument?

- the way he uses language to identify with his hearers (see verses 17, 26, 32)?
- How would you summarise the main point of Paul's argument?
- Why doesn't Paul immediately talk about Jesus?
- When Paul does come to talk about Jesus what does he focus on?
- Does Paul use warnings or promises in his speech?
- What is Paul's goal in this speech – to inform or to persuade?

b) Read **Acts 17:18–33**.

The background to this passage is that, while waiting in Athens for Silas and Timothy, Paul not only speaks in the synagogue to Jews but also addresses the Greek philosophers.

Paul was a Jew which meant that when he spoke in a synagogue, he was playing 'a home match', the main debating chamber in Athens, however, was very much an 'away game'.

- Looking at Paul's introduction in verses 22 and 23, how does he identify links with his Athenian hearers?
- Summarise Paul's argument in his speech.
- What things are present in this speech which show that Paul is building bridges with his listeners?
- How is this speech similar to Paul's speech to the Jews of Pisidian Antioch recorded in Acts 13?
- What differences are there with the speech in Antioch?
- What lessons are there here for us about preaching with persuasion?

Power

The Bible makes it plain that sharing the good news of Jesus is a work that requires power. For one thing, conversion involves a person being brought miraculously from death to life and from darkness to light. For another, we face spiritual opposition as we share Jesus with people.

We looked at the Holy Spirit in Study Three; here we want to look at the way that he provides power for sharing the good news of Jesus.

a) As the pattern for someone who shares God's good news, Jesus was himself filled with God's power. In **Acts 10:38** we read a concise summary of Jesus' ministry:

- How is Jesus described here?
- What is the relevance of the mention of the Holy Spirit in this brief description?

b) Read **Acts 1:8**.

Put yourself in the disciples' position; you have probably never travelled more than fifty miles from your place of birth, you have recently messed up in Jerusalem. You are now being ordered to be a witness for him to the ends of the earth.

+ What would you be thinking?
+ When you think about sharing your faith today do you share those concerns?

c) Read the following verses in Acts. Decide briefly what task or function the Holy Spirit is performing in each instance.

Acts 2:16–18; Acts 9:31; Acts 10:44–47; Acts 13:9–11; Acts 15:28; Acts 16:7; Acts 20:22–23

Praise

The original meaning of the English word 'praise' was to appraise or to set a price on something. 'Worship' has a similar root; it originally meant worth-ship; it was to express the worth or value of something. To praise or worship God means to express his value or worth to us. And that is a witness in itself.

a) Read **Psalm 150**.

+ Why is the Lord to be praised?
+ How is he to be praised?
+ Who and what is to praise the Lord?

b) At the heart of the Old Testament worship system was sacrifice. As Jesus is the fulfilment of the sacrifice for our sins, what do we offer in place of a sacrifice in our worship?

Read **Romans 12:1**.

+ What would it mean for our lives to be living sacrifices?

Patterning

Bringing people to know Christ is not the end of the story; it is just the beginning. The New Testament is full of instructions on how new believers are to be discipled so that they grow up into maturity. They are to be given a pattern for how they are to live.

a) Read **Matthew 28:18–20** again.

- Does Jesus tell his followers to go and make converts? What is the difference between a convert and a disciple? (Hint: the word 'discipline' comes from the same root as 'disciple'.)
- What does Jesus say that new followers are to be taught?

b) Read **Philippians 3:17–21**.

- On the basis of this passage what do you consider was the danger faced by the Christians in Philippi?
- What rule does Paul give them in verse 17?
- Could we honestly say to new Christians 'pattern your life after mine'?

EVALUATION

Persuasion

Why do you think that Christians are often so unpersuasive about sharing their faith? Is it because

- They don't believe what they are saying?
- They don't make the Christian life seem very appealing?
- They don't relate to where people are at?

Power

- What strengths and abilities other than the power of the Holy Spirit might we rely on?
- Do we actually depend on the Holy Spirit to help us in our work as witnesses?

Praise

- Does our personal and church worship adequately reflect the value that we place on God?
- If someone who was not a Christian visited your church, during the worship time would something of God's worth and value be communicated to them?

Patterning

- A conversion to Christ is a new birth and is wonderful. It does however only produce a new-born infant. What is the ultimate goal that we should be working and praying for?
- How do you feel about those who make a Christian commitment and then, after a while lose interest? Is it always their fault?
- If converts to Christ can be discipled so that they in turn can lead others to Christ, then church growth can be explosive. Starting with '1' go round the group with each person doubling the number given by the person to their right – 1, 2, 4, 8, etc. This, of course, is just one person helping to generate one other conversion. When you get more than one new believer produced the growth rate is even more spectacular.

EXPRESSION

Persuasion

- Is your (or your church's) mission addressing the questions that you think people are asking, rather than the questions that they are really asking?
- How can you be more persuasive?
- Are you making good use of the evangelistic resources – books, tapes, videos and live events such as music, theatre and mission meetings, that are available?

Power

- At what stage of evangelism does the Holy Spirit become necessary? Is there any stage where the Holy Spirit is not involved?
- How can we rely more on the Holy Spirit to help us in our work as witnesses?

Praise

- If someone who was not a believer came into church and heard bored and apathetic worship what would they think of God?
- How can we improve our worship and praise to better reflect God's glory and worth?
- How can we praise God outside the church? Can we worship him in how we work, rest and play?

Patterning

- Why do people tend to neglect making disciples out of converts?
- What procedures can you put in place in a church to ensure that effective discipling goes on?
- How would you feel if you found out that someone was patterning themselves after you?

And finally . . .

- Which of these last four pillars is the one that you feel that God most wants to build up in you?
- What situations might you face this week in which you can put into practice some of the truths you have learnt together?
- How can you best support one another in your witness?
- Reviewing the course, what three things would you like to implement in your witness?
- Pray once again in small groups for the seven people that you have been praying for during this course.

Conclude by saying together **Psalm 67**.

Final Word

I do hope you have been encouraged and equipped to be more effective by these studies. Efficiency is doing things right; effectiveness is doing right things. Therefore play your part so that evangelism can be:

* Continuous: let it go on all the time (Acts 2:47).
* Congregational: let the whole church be mobilized (John 20:21).
* Caring: let it be demonstrated by love and sensitivity to people's needs (1 Thessalonians 2:7–8).
* Conserving: let each new believer grow spiritually and become active (Colossians 1:28–29).

A friend of mine, Dr Leighton Ford, wrote:

Jesus was born in a borrowed manger.
He preached from a borrowed boat.
He entered Jerusalem on a borrowed donkey.
He ate the Last Supper in a borrowed upper room.
He was buried in a borrowed tomb.
Now he asks to borrow the lives of Christians to reach the rest of the world.
If we do not speak, then he is dumb and silent.

God gives us the boat and the oars, but then tells us, 'It's up to you to row!'
So row and take risks. Remember, if Michelangelo hadn't taken risks he would have painted the floor of the Sistine Chapel!
I know it is often hard to be a Christian, but it would be too dull to be anything else. A missionary is not someone who crosses the sea; a missionary is someone who sees the Cross.
May the love of Christ, demonstrated when he died on the Cross, compel you with a Resurrection and eternal message.